Big Machines at Sea

Geoff Thompson

Contents

Ships	4
Sailing the seas	8
Ocean liners	10
Submarines	12
Cargo ships	14
Hovercraft	16
Ferries	18
Aircraft carriers	20
The Sailing Ship	23
Questions	24
Glossary	24
Index	25

Ships

There are many kinds of ships.

ocean liner

container ship

aircraft carrier

Ships can carry very big loads across the sea.

Ships are much bigger than boats.
The first ships and boats were made of wood.
Some of them had sails.

Now ships are made of steel.
They have engines
to help them move through the water.

Ships and boats long ago...

These boats had one big sail and were used for long trips.

early Egyptian boats

Longboats were made of wood. They were very strong in heavy seas.

Viking longboats

These ships had many sails and could go a long way across the sea.

sailing ships

Ships today...

Ocean liners are much faster than sailing ships.
They use engines.

These ships take huge loads from one place to another.

Submarines are ships that can go under the sea.

Sailing the seas

Long ago, sailing ships
were the only way to cross the sea.

Painting of an old sailing ship

These ships had sails to catch the wind.
The wind blew into the sails.
This pushed the ship forwards.

Sailing ships could not move
if there was no wind.

Ocean liners

Today, ocean liners carry lots of people across the sea.

People go for holidays at sea on ocean liners.

Ocean liners have many cabins. Cabins are small rooms where people sleep.

Ocean liners have swimming pools and shops. Some have play rooms for children, too.

Submarines

A submarine is a ship that can go deep down under the sea.

Submarines can float on top of the water, too.

Submarines can move quickly
through the water,
because they are long and thin
and have round ends.

DID YOU KNOW?

Some submarines
can stay under the water
for up to 60 days.

Cargo ships

Cargo ships take big loads
from one place to another.

This cargo ship is a container ship.
Containers are loaded onto the ship.
They are full of all kinds of cargo.

This cargo ship
is an oil tanker.
Oil tankers
are very long.
Inside,
they have big tanks
filled with oil.

DID YOU KNOW?

Some oil tankers are so long that sailors have to ride a bike to get from one end to another.

Hovercraft

A hovercraft is a special kind of ship. It can go over water and up onto land.

A hovercraft sits on a huge air cushion.

Propellers on top of the hovercraft help to push it forward.

Big hovercraft take people on short, fast trips across the sea.

Ferries

Ferries take people on trips across rivers and bays. Sometimes they go across the sea from one island to another.

Some big ferries carry cars and trucks.
The cars and trucks
go in through big doors
at one end of the ferry.
They are parked in a special place
called a hold.

Aircraft carriers

Aircraft carriers are very big ships. Planes can take off and land from the runway on aircraft carriers.

DID YOU KNOW?

Some aircraft carriers can hold about 50 planes.

The Sailing Ship

We have sailed on our ship
For many long weeks,
Over the rolling sea.
And down in the cabins
We have heard the wind
Blowing strong and free.

The captain takes us
On and on,
Until, one sunny day,
The ship that has been
Our home on the waves
Comes sailing into the bay.

Jenny Giles

Questions

1. How long can some submarines stay under the water?

2. What do sailors sometimes do to get from one end of an oil tanker to the other?

3. How many planes can some aircraft carriers hold?

Glossary

container	*a large tank for storing goods*
hold	*the place where cargo is put inside a ship*
propeller	*a set of spinning blades that pushes a boat or plane forwards*
runway	*the place where planes take off and land.*